Drawing the Shade

poems by

MICHAEL ROTHENBERG

Illustrations by Donatella D'Angelo

DOS MADRES

2016

DOS MADRES PRESS INC.
P.O.Box 294, Loveland, Ohio 45140
www.dosmadres.com   editor@dosmadres.com

Dos Madres is dedicated to the belief that the small press is essential
to the vitality of contemporary literature as a carrier of the new voice,
as well as the older, sometimes forgotten voices of the past. And in an
ever more virtual world, to the creation of fine books pleasing to the
eye and hand.

Dos Madres is named in honor of Vera Murphy and Libbie Hughes,
the "Dos Madres" whose contributions have made this press possible.

Dos Madres Press, Inc. is an Ohio Not For Profit Corporation and a
501 (c) (3) qualified public charity. Contributions are tax deductible.

Executive Editor: Robert J. Murphy

Illustration & Book Design: Elizabeth H. Murphy
www.illusionstudios.net

Typset in Adobe Garamond Pro & Adine Kirnberg
ISBN 978-1-939929-56-3
Library of Congress Control Number: 2016938881

First Edition

ACKNOWLEDGEMENTS

Excerpts from these journals have previously appeared in *Otoliths, Poets' Corner, Exquisite Corpse, Fulva flava, Gulf Stream, Jack, Jujitsu with others #1, Madhatter's Review, Wandering Hermit Review, Dead Drunk Dublin, La Bloga, Papertiger, Small Town,* and *88: A Journal of Contemporary American Poetry.* "Grown Up Cuba" was first published as a chapbook by Il Begatto Press, Amsterdam (editor, Louise Landes Levi). "The Jet" from "Drawing The Shade" was first published in *Choose* (Big Bridge Press) and recorded on the CD "Under The Spell" by Michael Rothenberg with Bobby Thomas Jr. in 2002.

Thanks to Joanne Kyger and David Meltzer for permission to reproduce selections of personal correspondence. Gratitude to Anselm Hollo for his generous insights.

for my Mother and Alex

1

Grown Up Cuba

for Joanne Kyger

Oh no, not another broken heart!

      Let Elian Gonzalez go home to his father
The regime of doing without and not having, speaking
    forbidden against the holy president and king

    sleeping under leaking tin, one vote, one voter, one
        party, one beer, just add six tear drops to
each night, clock, day watch, work week

           moment, pulse, root, tendril, claw
    assassin. Recite this bone-faced prayer
      and a cup of silence becomes sacred wine

What you don't say . . .what she doesn't hear . . .

     *

    "Date it!"

   Somehow, I left off the date (this place)
     when I excerpted

       the poem from
       the poem

    *

More Instructions from Another Side

*

I dream I found a note pad someone left on an airplane
I begin writing but I don't remember what

*

Ash Wednesday

Think of an ash enso
        Walk down 5th Ave. to Suzi's

    office of Poetry and day trading on the 34th floor
        Talk business, Buddha, abstraction, fashion and inheritance

*

I meet Wanda
at Café della Artistes on Greenwich

Chocolate cake, diet cola
We exchange publications and tapes

She doesn't like something I say
Calls me a dick

I tell her to shut up and fuck off
I'm out of control

She pays her tab and walks out
She's out of control

We make up on the sidewalk
"Where's Cuba?"

*

"eyes like drenched violets"

Orlando, Virginia Woolf

*

Peanut butter sesame bagel, diet cola
1:30 a.m.

New trends in poetry, an idea
of poetry as fashion—

a horrifying mindset

"It's anxiety/depression."

Queens night skyline blasts across the river
Suzi and I drink ginger ale

*

CUBACUBACUBACUBACUBACUBA

1:30 a.m., March 13, Miami, Florida

*

Gale winds, Jacuzzi bubbles at 102 degrees
White cap swimming pool, small craft warning

Miami

Black beans & rice

3

*

Headlines

USA Today: "GROWING UP IN CUBA"

*

Bus stop green low-rider Impala boom box idling

*

Joanne took Ritalin as a kid. She tried to get some
in Japan. They made her sign a paper
"This is a drug!" They said

*

"I try to call you but your phone is always busy" Joanne says

My phone always needs new batteries

"I just need an assignment from you   to know when we should begin
But feelings   expressed in letters seem so personal   and finite
they frighten me.   After all,   the feelings we have on one day
are exactly that.   There's nothing   we could *ever* say
that we could *always* mean.   Is there?"

*

Depression, reoccurring kung pao chicken
Disassociation. The Academy Awards

So many good things

going on despite high prices at the pumps

4

I send out a poem like a filet of raw nerve

                    Is it performance anxiety?

          I've got money problems, lease instability
          I don't feel close to anyone
I can't even imagine what would feel good
     So much fattening or habit forming
                    Chocolate cake

                    and Valium

Nothing can be solved
     Put it to bed and try   try to wake up

          in the morning

          work harder, workaholic, mail, write, invent

but I feel like   killing myself

                    though even that

                              lacks any promise of gratification

                    I'd expect

          from making a clean sweep

     Brush

                    But it's a different kind of suicidal thought

                    Sweep

*

(see Joanne's *The Japan and India Journals*)

Go through her journals for her Selected Poems (*As Ever*)

"Letter to Nemi Frost"

"Anne Waldman already *used* that
        but whatever
            it is
                    should be part of

                        the overall texture.

        Just make notes."

                *

Bolinas and back

I read a Pat Nolan travel journal   Joanne remembers hosting
        a library poetry reading

        Beer on the rip rap
        Later a mesa party

Rolling Stone interview about the late Richard Brautigan

                *

I see that night is now upon me, my arms and hair

What I did know
How I did it

But there we were

You have to remind me

*

Joanne says:
"Keep a journal, a notebook by the phone."

*

Treadmill Telephone Call Memory

"I'm not going to *talk* to you if you're going to talk to *me*
while you're walking on *that*."

*

Double Rainbow
Storm   blue black silver clouds

Good Fortune or Danger?
I feel them both

Hurry up kids!
Get out of the pool!

Splash, screams
Raindrops on sunglasses

It could be as easy as going   inside
But why hide from the perils of beauty?

So I go downstairs to get closer
It disappears

     *

   "It's great

       things are timeless but

     I was talking about someone's death . . ."

  On the mesa

     or that flower bowing over the fence
         onto the path

  from Dennis Breedlove's
  insane Chiapas garden

     *

  Linda Russo is working on a feature about Joanne and Philip
    for *Jacket* magazine

       I explain the difficulty
I have writing about people as things
     It's difficult to summarize anyone that . . .

  "Academic." Joanne says

  Right, so I want to find a phrase, a Latin phrase
    like *caveat emptor* to put at the end, to keep
     the people and flowers open

meaning this is what I think
today   only it might change

in another moment

"There's a whole bunch of good ones
like *cogito ergo sum.*"

Or something that means   we know we don't *know,* but in Latin

*

"In the beginner's mind there are many possibilities;
in the expert's mind there are few."
– Shunryu Suzuki

*

"Compulsive about dates"

Editing, she puts out only careful arrangements
Ikebana
Spicer and Duncan putter around with clippers and scissors
in baseball caps and Martha Stewart bibs

I'm going to Miami where pink hibiscus and gold anthers grow

"Go to Cuba!"

*

A 250 page journal assignment from Joanne

*

Someone said that between you and Philip it seemed
I was editing the whole

CANON

"Oh, the canon, yes, *el canon*, that's better
than *la pistola*."

*

Buy a cigar, do the rumba down on Deco Dr.
South Beach
      where gramps ran numbers

from Carlyle to Carlton

"It's good Ricky Martin didn't win
what do you call it the . . ."

Grammies…

Oh, that Latin fever in the drum

"for his cheesy hip-swinging . . .on TV . . ."

La Vida Loca

"Isn't it the truth!"

*

Blue skies, white clouds
A lady sits beside me with one earplug
The airplane lands

Blue bay
Speedboat aquaplaning
White brushstroke wake
Follows the inboard /outboard motor roar

*

Cubans, I grew up with them, Miami, The Bay of Pigs
They never bothered me

Paradise is always up for grabs
The song of my youth

Why should I be the last hotshot rocket top-down in palm-town?

"That was part of your life? I didn't know about that!
It explains your style . . ."

*

I knew one day I'd get something wrong, trip up on the way
with Joanne, sooner or later

in my hurry to approach

the imbalance of iris and cherry blossom

spiking and curved
against obsession
But, I don't think I did

*

"Keep a journal.
Paragraphs beginning with big letters—
CUBA!"

11

*

Vernal Equinox

Pack bags
Send mail
Eat bagel
Buy sponge
Call California
Count my lucky stars
Edit a poem

On the balcony
Watch bay clouds
Nobody belongs anywhere

A few people knew me
A few people know me

Make plans
Schedule love
Between work and family
All said and done

*

I ask the Roshi how to get rid of obsession
He says, "Burn incense"

                                    Check space and dates
                                    Don't be an autocrat!

So I burn incense and nothing happens
Only the smoke vanishes

Then, I knock over a vase in too much of a hurry to be
done and correct

The broken flesh
The celadon glaze

*

"Cuidado."

I've got my passport

    "You're going to Miami, that's the good son thing to do
    But you should go to CUBA!

    Keep a journal, I'll leave you notes on your
                        answering machine."

My mother has emphysema. I can't take care of that

    "CUBA!!"

Okay, Cuba
What about Cuba?

      Crazy with the reflection at a later day, for Cuba

A contract comes in with a nice letter from Paul Slovak

    About when we should begin
          working on editing Joanne's book

    "CUBA!!!"

Maybe I *will* go, not a bad idea.

      Cuba!

    Dragging the phone cord

13

around the room

stepping on curly wires, my curly mind

in the jeweler's cabinet where I keep my   recent thoughts

I've got my passport
right here

"Pues, Adios!"

February 23-March 31, 2000

2

17

Drawing the Shade

I

Clothes piled up in the driveway
We depart in chaos, sadness and anger

I-95 south of Richmond, Virginia

Can't find the right road on
Can't find the right road off

Going to Miami with my son to see my mother

The Goddess shovels coal silently

*

Cotton fields

Cosmos says
"Well, who says a father and son can't bond?"

*

Washington, D.C, 8:30 p.m.

Capitol Building
Washington Monument
Jefferson Memorial

LIT UP

Excited, we drive all around
Stop to sleep in Econo Lodge

I call Lakshmi

while Cosmos is in the shower
To tell her I'm thinking about her
And that I'm sorry

The phone's busy
I call her maybe 20 times
Then I go to sleep

                *

7:30 a.m.

Doughnuts from the lobby

                *

Stop at a truck stop to call Lakshmi again
She cries on the telephone

It's not easy to know what to do

        The Goddess shovels coal silently

                *

Abandonment
Capitol Buildings

War, War, War

Everywhere
Cotton Fields

                    *

"What does it explain, Dad?"

    "Are we there yet, Dad?"

        "How many more hours to go?"

It doesn't explain anything I guess

                        12:55 November 3rd

                    *

(APOLOGY TO THE GODDESS)

Don't be angry
I tried to stay with you, be patient, wait, manage,
control my grief
Be everything to Mother and Goddess
But I couldn't

    Does that explain it?

I should have been with my mother
Been the good son
But I met you
        after looking so long for a life of poetry,
                    song and dance

You never said don't go
but feared I'd become my mother's death

The Goddess shovels coal silently

II

"Write it down," my mother says

Air-conditioning fan startles

"Write everything down, okay?"

Dipa, nurse from Gujrata, India brings morphine
Her name means The Light of The Flame

"Remember. Then what? What next?
The next thing, I forgot. The next thing
What's the next thing? Can I have some water?"

"No, not until the surgery's over," I say

"I forgot"

"Are you going to give me material for a poem, mom?"

"I forget. Where's the water? I forget"

"You forget a lot"

"It's hard to hold on to thoughts"

"I'm here to remember what you can't.
So where's that smiley face gone?"

"I can't remember. I'm gonna forget everything."
Never again. Never going to look good again"

"You still have those baby blue eyes"

She looks at me and smiles

"Write it down," she says, "I was the best fisherman in the family"

November 8, 2001

III

Thursday, Nov. 8, 2001

Dear Joanne,

Here it is Thursday and my mother is home from the hospital and
under hospice care. She's hardly conscious but we had some clarity
the first day at home. So that was a gift. I've made as many preparations
as I can imagine need to be made. Years ago I knew it was going to happen
this way. I am that person in my family. Nancy is coming to town on
Saturday and my brother on Sunday, so I will have some help (?) then.
I don't know if my mother will last the day. We have been to the
Hospital, (hell) and back. A blood clot in the leg and failed attempts to
dislodge it. Enough measures! The cancer and the emphysema already
taking her away. She's home and without pain . . .

Love to you and Donald,
Michael

*

Orange sunset lavender clouds

IV

~~I have come up to you~~
~~hold me in your arms~~

oh Mother, ~~don't send me back~~
~~I have come up to you~~

~~hold me in your arms~~
~~you will give me refuge~~

~~I have no other desire~~
~~I have no other craving~~

~~but to call you,~~ Mother
~~and sit at your feet~~

~~where else will I find a home?~~
~~here in deepest night~~

Mother, ~~I have come up to you~~
~~hold me in your arms~~

V

Cosmos' Dream

"I'm sitting in a room with grandma
in her bedroom
      It smelled weird
The cot was tilted, floating halfway up
Her skin orangey, yellow and blue
      with weird lines going through
      the center of her arms
      The curtains were slightly red with light
      coming through them
She was screaming, 'I'm rotting here'"

      "Then I'm in this gold room
        Gold shiny bathroom
              The cot still floating
                A tilted lamp on top of the sink cabinet
                    with a red floodlight in it
              On one side you could
              see through the wall into a hospital
        I could see a person walking down a hall
      wearing white
In the gold room
            her body was perfectly regular
She was still talking
'I'm in deep pain'
She was talking really weird
Her eyes hardly open . . ."

November 13

27

VI

November 13, 2001

Dear Michael,

'For 30 days the bereaved may not cut their hair, pare their
nails, wear new clothes, listen to music, celebrate weddings, go
to parties, appear at public gatherings, or visit places of enter-
tainment.' So it went in the old days (daze) but how it goes
nowadays is more like the delirium you described. All of it cha-
otic — an alternate universe w/weird background sonic static
of the shift. Where am I? But also elevated beyond anything
other than this crucial event, this major loss. What's important
is what remains. One is out of the usual orbit whether it's a
birth or death — &, in a sense, that's where we shd always be.
Deep embrace & tenderness. PS. thinking about your words on
'suffering' & am impressed w/ yr recognizing how tough & re-
sistant the organism is, despite all the misery, to checking out.
When do we get the clue to 'checking in'? Or is that irrelevant?

Love,
David Meltzer

    *

Where are you going to spend eternity?

    Quickly eroded in the face of mounting fears

    *

You can't let others speak for you
That's not an adequate expression of pain

The Goddess dances for love
The dance is much improved

Halloween pumpkin turned black and retired to the field
Lost all its teeth but still smiling

I tried to get to a place today
where I could describe the Biscayne Bay

Goodbye Miami!

In the Jacuzzi crying for my mother

October 20-November 17, 2001

VII

I'm too emotional to see anyone
Decorum doesn't mean squat
I buy broccoli and cook it alone

If you let me be myself and ask nothing of me
Don't pick up the phone when it rings
You can come share the broccoli with me

I was raised to be transparent
In bed, no lover wonders if my mind is
Somewhere else. They know

My mother lies between lovers and poetry
To make sure I am respectful

I want to be anonymous. Invisible
So I'm painting the clear plastic
Window to my world with a rainbow
From the inside

In the future you will have to
Ask me where I'm at
Maybe I'll tell you

November 23, 2001

VIII

I'm in North Miami on Biscayne Bay, ninth floor facing southeast
I watch the sunrise in the morning and the sunset at night,
from silver to pink on a daily basis. Miami is not laid back and
the hippie scene is all but lost in the paralysis of self analysis
looking for a stylish step in a twelve step internet program for
enlightenment. Words have become more significant than
deeds, grace and generosity are part of a program to bolster the
American economy, and cynicism is at an all time low due to the fact
that idealism is out of fashion. Idealism is a television program
not a passion, so I'm resigned to the truth of the tides and
the movement of clouds, and evidence of life after death in the
telecasting of Sally Jesse Raphael and Jerry Springer. After all,
desperate living IS what living is about. Breast implants and
a preoccupation with flesh isn't so bad when you think of the
alternative: zomboids, western guilt, eastern shame, denial and
genital alienation. Regarding my Pennsylvania schedule,
I've cancelled my tickets and will stay here in Miami until
whatever storm it is that's blowing in a new life has completed
tearing up the old by the roots and no longer threatens to
crush my skull with it's charitable exercise. So I won't be
going back to PA and will be going to Pacifica as soon as I get
the urge. And that's the way things seem to be happening
I sit and drink coffee, then get the urge to go toast a bagel
Then I'm back at my typewriter thinking I want to live here forever
looking at the bright blue bay, when before I know it the realtor
is knocking at the door with a contract to list the apartment
for sale, the result of a phone call from me that came from an urge
I forgot I had

IX

The fortune teller says buy a blue sapphire ring
Give the man sandalwood beads blessed by a Buddhist

monk. And if you're missing pieces pictured in the
assembly instructions, or the box for your model airplane

includes an extra adornment, chrome spoke or
insignia, and you can't just leave it alone to fit together

later when things make more sense, like when your
mother dies, or volcanoes on Io erupt like Daisy Cutters

in holy wars against Aladdin, then lash yourself
with stinging nettles, annihilate the ballroom mirror,

let marble halls, Royal Palm gardens, bubbling swimming
pools, teak elephants from Thailand in the lobby

of the palace, and The Doorman turn into a pillar of salt and
blow away. Crawl on the roadside under Saturn's light

in tears of icy blue-collar shame, shame, looking
for what you threw away, console yourself in the eyes

of always transient devotees, you'll need to do that,
explain yourself to them for this mistaken identification,

in order to have a meaningful script for your next
missionary expedition to enlighten pre-adolescent

Punjabi soldiers, explain yourself for having strayed into a
romance with an adult male, or you can leave this part out,

your politically/socially foolish cares. Do pujas, become a
renunciate, never seen or really understood by anyone

X

"The only second chance I know is to make the same mistake twice."

—David Mamet

Responder

Someday we can be friends
Death and pink hibiscus

Happy Hanukah, 5th day
Latke party at shul for singles

Or remain suspended in a
teenage fury, wind

whirling flames, cob-webbed
arrested development, sculptured

tortured stunted roots clinging to religion
carried too far from it's source to nurture

without Miracle Grow

Good morning
But no reply speaking to my eye

Soundlights float, beat side to side
In hunger taste is mute

I eat asparagus fern
Birth and sinking blue-gray folds

"Blessed art thou . . ."

The mortuary wants to know
What I want inscribed on the vault:

"I'm sorry I could not wave a wand
across the gasping face of ivory pain

But I know we're in this for the same
reason. I doubt there's more

than one Ultimate Display"
Birth date. Death date

Written before in a poem scored for a radio play
Jitterbug & The Good Ship Lollipop

December 13, 2001

XI

Mystery Squid
Ghostly in ink black frigid ocean waters three miles below
Small head topped by fleshy, collar-like fins
10 wispy appendages coated in sticky mucous
             stretch out for 20ft, dangle to entrap small prey

Magnapinna (bigfin) *pacifica*

The only planet in our solar system that rotates
clockwise

VENUS

If anything enters its atmosphere
        it is immediately
               crushed

Underneath thick cloud cover
                    active volcanoes and sulfuric acids

Its days last longer than its years

Shekinah- Isvari, Mystery Squid on planet Venus
for a stable reflection. Where were you tonight

when the sheets of brine unfolded white
over your black wavy hair, green eyes, and sugar tongue?

Lying there looking past my skull through the ceiling?
Where were you? Thinking your way through?

Beyond what wire fence or vast cosmic dictatorship?
Did you get there, on the other side of things?

Or will you have to go back to the start, like any
ordinary person with the same map and questions

Hands probing your liquefying divinity for grace

XII

The jet is now perceived as a weapon
The boat is now perceived as a weapon
The house, a weapon
The car, a weapon

The tree
The toy
The air

Vehicles for poison, explosives
Film, magazine, song, propaganda

What can't be used for killing is frivolous

One drop of water is one holy jihad

Seeds of love in your enemy's heart
Walk away!

Security is perceived as a weapon
Fidelity is perceived as a weapon

Prayer, a weapon
Goddess, a weapon
Vegetarian cuisine
Yoga, a weapon

     Art & religion in the hands of a villain is black magic

Orgasm, a weapon
Nation, a weapon
The tribe, the hive, location is a weapon

Now I've got the money to travel beyond time
But no place is safe the weapon is mind

XIII

Concrete sky and stars
Seagrape & sand barrier islands

Have I lost faith or is this grace?

Follow me down, Mother
I am never alone

Green pelicans and Hare Krishna
Some stranger's hand

Or pink sequined perfume
You know that's plenty

December 30, 2001

XIV

Somewhere between
Russian movies and grief counseling

A shitty haze hangover from sleep medication
It can get worse

My bed is in the hall
Looking for a Kuan Yin in a sleigh bell

An antler hat

Sending Sermons from The Mount by Priority Mail
In a red Santa cap

Kneading the edge of the blanket up around
My chin

Anxious festivities
Goofy expectations of New Year's

Celebrations. Gyrations
A happy face makes me want to scream

The bargain sale holiday rush to flocked wrappings
Satin ribbons & bows

Greetings!
Now draw the shade.

January 21, 2001

3

THE MAN INSIDE

I

One day I walk inside the head of a buddha
And there is a man inside
Completely articulate
Talking to me
And I'm listening

> *We live double lives*
> *Everyone does*
> *Public & private self*

> *When private self is*
> *lost in its direction*
> *public self spins out*
> *of control*

> *A sheet of paper*
> *torn in the wind*

*

We're having a conversation

Philip calls to tell me
he doesn't think he can keep
his promise to live longer than me

*

New Smyrna Beach walk, gossip, seafood & a bottle of wine
Giacometti & Zhivago shadows on moonlit estuary
A strip club w/ Anne Waldman

5/25/2002

*

I speak to Ellie
The Jockey Club security guard at the mail delivery dock
about the pretty woman I saw in the building
and ask her to introduce us
Ellie gives the woman a call

"So what do you think, Ellie?"
"If I were single I'd date him," Ellie says

"That's so sweeeet," she says
"Yes, he didn't want to interfere with your privacy
So he asked me to talk to you. He's shy. A writer
He wears his hair in a ponytail"

"That's so cute" she says
"But now it's up to you. I wouldn't wait
You have to take chances in life
Do you want to call him?"
"Yes, but it could be two days or two weeks
        That's how I am"

It might as well be never

*

Tropical blue sky and train whistle
Where's it all going?

It might as well be the last place on earth

    *

  I want a tailor to make me some special clothes
   Dressy and comfortable
      Some fancy pajamas for this isolation

    *

Unplug the telephone
Keep the bathroom clean
Write. Write. Write
And eventually end up dead on the floor
clutching an empty tuna fish can

  A tradition
  Woe is me
  I can't even bring happiness to a birth!

  People create
  a family. And it goes on. Then it dies

  ALL AT ONCE

      OH, Philip, don't
  die today

  I'm good at sitting shiva
  But I've lost my sense of humor

I walk on the treadmill
The same old treadmill

A guy repairs his car horn
9 floors down
It keeps blowing in my poem

*

Underground Academy
7:30 Lincoln Rd. w/ Beth Lagaron, she writes
about William Burroughs, wants to get a paper published
but most magazines that publish articles which enable
students to become successful professors, to get
jobs, don't publish articles about

William Burroughs

Or Jack Kerouac

*

Luna Star Café Hangout #1

It's this unfolding thing unrealized like
I'm dying

NOW

Oh, oh, oh, baby!

I haven't written my last poem yet

*

I invited you to come

Take the day off

No, you *can't* have my penis!

May 22, 2002

*

There's a Train
I keep falling off the tracks

Fix your fucking alarm
I'm trying to write a poem

I need   SILENCE!!

*

Giselle
Is that her name?
Blonde, cute, 2 daughters, single
Living in the same building
Is that looking too close?

II

Doves as loud as any bird or
caterpillar tearing up the road, back up
    beeper blaring

OH, what sounds
we choose to punish ourselves with

Anne Waldman whispers to get attention
We all do

A Whisper of Humanity

Whisper of war on the border, one million soldiers flexing
nuclear muscles, Hindus & Muslims

How prophetic. GOD ENDS

THE WORLD. He started it/ he can
finish it

              *

    Got another   Goodbye Letter   from the Dancer

              *

    DANCING MINDLESSNESS

    You can't separate your ego from your dancing

Time to get rid of the dancer

*

O, Dates!

*

An anchor
Just to know where we are in our lives

*

"Please don't write back"

Organization is what keeps me alive

Circles

Small Steps

Fold in upon themselves

Folding them in

She refuses to be kind

*

Is this another love poem?

Yes, a political love poem

Are you reading tonight?

No, I'm watching

Ceramic cat sitting on chair hung from the wall

*

Got a divorce lawyer

      Got another   Goodbye Letter   from The Dancer

*

It's only Monday
Everyone says no to someone
Should I ask Giselle out?
I'm incredibly shy
Re-enact the many roles my mother played
Two crows in black clouds
I swore I'd never live in a condominium

You can't waste time. You have to say,

      "'Scuse me, boootiful. Ya lookin' for a boyfriend?"

        No, I'm not another guy come to fuck you over

        I've just been paying close attention

        Now listen

*

      Dream meet woman

      Woman meet dream

*

I'm in Miami
Noisy sun and bay

Day after day
I don't even know

Why I'm doing it
Fighting with people

Because I'm tired

But YOU GOT LAMPS!!

Lamps will keep you up at night

*

Oh, Love!

That's all you can do

The rest belongs to the Government

5/12/2002

III

I suffered a great deal because of my refusal to play by the rules
A Hellion

    now

Who's that man inside the buddhahead?
Talking to me?

      You can't expect to know
          where you're going

          while you're going
               there

Here. Here!

     *

      Go away lover girl
      Become another one

     of the
   Lost & Found

so I don't have to think about you anymore

     *

       It's Sunday
       Giselle hasn't called
       Why should she call?
       My friends say she won't call

I'll have to run into her in the lobby
And start a polite conversation

Don't be so fucking impatient!

You have to cope with the vibrations
No matter where you are

Somewhere

*

Leaf blowers
Chain saws

Noisy hot tropics

*

Get up and go
You're limited by your imagination
Get a rich young wife

Live forever . . .

*

And the like

*

Meet Luke and Giselle
Luke, is a messenger from god
Giselle, is Aphrodite

*

Oh my god!
Nicole Kidman's single
I should call her up and ask her for a date

*

Get up and go

May 19, 2002

You're limited by your imagination
Get a rich young wife
Live forever

Waiting for that call
I get in bed, get stoned
It'll work out

WARNING: Don't watch T.V. alone

*

Who will come for me?
Save me from this awful Death of Luxury?
Unemployed with a steady income
Where does poetry come from?
Where is that woman who will love me forever?

*

Wallflower Gallery

Finally, I get out

What am I yelling about?

Some New Age Jazz

Electronic bamboo wind-pipes
Even robots don't breathe like that

IV

One Good Woman

Just one good woman, please!

*

Lincoln Rd. Mall 45 years later
Oriental Chicken Salad
Italian waiter
91° under the umbrella
Rhythm & Blues Brazilian style
Bulldogs in Argentinian cowboy hats

*

Dead fucking calm
Drink coffee, read the papers, watch T.V. news
Wonder what Giselle is doing 7 floors below

*

Smoked salmon, whitefish
Swiss cheese, bagels, sliced tomatoes
Cole slaw, egg salad brunch

Waking slowly, the whole day long worrying
about what I might miss if I don't go out

So much flesh and pearls
Sweat, to drool upon
without a chance of a kiss

Falling into the lap of pre-Monday anxiety,

what I must do to make a whole life complete,
   books I could read

   The pressure of undertaking ambition

      Noon by the pool with the same 6 people
      The Venezuelan who sells diamonds on the internet
      His hot wife in the pink thong bikini
      Their three kids
      Their Venezuelan neighbor from next door

The Doctor who stitched up my glass torn face when I was 3
Who took care of my father through three heart attacks
and two strokes steps into the pool

      Speaking to myself
      Looking around for my mother
      who should be here but is dead
      and still talking to me

            *

   Lhasa Tibetan Restaurant Poetry Reading
w/ LLL in NYC, June 15th in garden room

      Angels, Apocalyptic Yearnings

            *

   MOTHER!

I need my mother!

You need a nurse

*

Because I know when I stop
I'll be in the middle of a noise
                that has nothing to do with me

*

Hurricane Season begins

*

                        Mother's little helper

*

Human contact is painful
Everything's got a clock

Electric power is always going out
Moloch is Mr. President

Your underwear is caught in your zipper

*

DRAMA QUEEN

*

Skipping stones

Hopping from where
they once were

Or from stone to stone

*

ANALOGY

An allergy

*

Rednecks in the White House

*

                                        Mama's gone

And the woman I thought I'd live my life with

*

Three women, they come in Holy Threes:

    The Disaster Queen
    The Russian Caviar
    The Chai

*

Addicted to innocence

    He likes younger women
    Uses conditioner, restorer, purifier to make
        a half head of hair silky

Romantic illusion debunked

May 19, 2002

V

Memorial Day

A beautiful day for tropical recreation

I can do it alone

*

      Go away!
You old lovers!
Give me time to think about myself
What's good for me
      It's my room!

        Oh, God!

        (in my room)

*

      Memorial Day
In the apartment I wait for the Jockey Club Barbecue
      Maybe I'll meet someone

  There

What's going on?

      Here again

I walk around the apartment
Talk to myself, to my mother, talk on the telephone

Maybe I won't talk to anyone anymore because
Nobody tells me what I want to hear

What is it you want to hear?

Ask my old lovers
The blonde, the redhead, the one with hair like a shawl
Specters!

Haunting, analyzing, categorizing
Getting me ready for grooming!
They take me into their arms
Hold me
Keep me around to worship them
Make me new for them
                    everyday!

Their little boy doll

                    *

Oh, dead lovers, living lovers, lost lovers gone, gone

            You sure know how to sit shiva

We've each got our very own style

                    *

Check the mail

The last woman who fell in love with me was a lesbian

            Why?

*

Oh

        It must be time to masturbate again!

*

Sundays are confusing

Does anyone know what I'm doing?

      I've contrived to conceive of popular love
as a spiritual matter

*

New Smyrna Beach Strip Club

"Who has the power? The man or the woman?" Anne says

If you take the tantric view it's a toss up
         dollar for dollar

*

Is it barbecue time?

I don't want to be alone
Ask anyone!

Is it barbecue time?
No, two and one half more hours

        Monday 4:01 p.m.

*

I forget what day it is
And realize it doesn't matter what day it is

*

Call Suzanne to guide me through
the perils of The Jockey Club Barbecue gathering
Maybe I'll meet someone there

*

May 29, 2002

Hallucinations are Hope

Mina Loy

Feeling was feeling you

*

It gets good in the end
People will stay
It just needs to be beautiful

*

Then something awful happens

JEOPARDY

To choose and not to be always chosen

May 31- June 2, 2002 11:16 a.m.

67

VI

Sunset in Miami wondering why Giselle still hasn't called
I imagine she's the woman serving me drinks
Or drinking with me

There ought to be tons of divorced women here!

*

I head out Monday morning 8:30 a.m. pretending to go to the post office
Just to see if I can accidentally, serendipitously
run into Giselle

No coffee. I shower and brush my teeth. A briefcase to make it official
Like clockwork she's aerobic walking down the palm-lined drive
wearing headphones, black tights working hard
Sweating in her long loose cotton blouse
I drive past her
Park the car
Sit in the lobby and wait for her

She comes in and races past me out of breath
into the open elevator and up to wherever it is she lives
I think the second floor

I ask Fred at the security desk
"What that lady's name?"
"Giselle," he says
"Is she single?"
"Yes"
"She lives on the second floor?"
"Yes"
"She's cute, isn't she?"
He gives me the thumbs up

*

"Why," my friends ask at dinner, "would she call you
if she doesn't remember seeing you? She'll never call." Sigh.
"You have to run into her. Introduce yourself. Get to know her"

I think I've heard this before
Said this before in an altered state

*

Look Luke, pull yourself together

Giselle loves to dance

"He loves me, he loves me not"

O, Lilies of the Tropics!

"unbridgeable gap between belief in simple happiness
of long ago places and the dark brooding
disaster of unattainable love"

Woman as Perfect and unattainable. Man is base. (Gautier)

Absolute Love devoid of sexual fulfillment

"Passion of enforced chastity"

Luke, you're getting ahead of yourself

"longed for a simple past"

*

The Story In A Nutshell

1. *Harvest time*
2. *Giselle, a happy innocent girl of 15*
3. *Hilarian, a gamesman in love with Giselle*
4. *Prince Albrecht, he stumbles upon her, spies upon her, he is enchanted*
5. *Albrecht disguises himself as Loy, a peasant, and woos her*
6. *Loy dances with Giselle, he swears his undying love*
7. *She loves me, she loves me not*
8. *Hilarian is jealous*
9. *Villagers return, declare Giselle The Village Queen*
10. *Giselle's mother warns her against dancing*
11. *Bathilda, Albrecht's arranged intended, is enchanted by Giselle's tale of love, she gives her a necklace*
12. *Hilarian discovers the sword and clothes, summons the party back*
13. *Bathilde is amused at Albrecht's dress. He calls it a whim*
14. *Giselle realizes betrayal, in delirium reprises the history of romance*
15. *Giselle goes crazy and dies*

ACT TWO Begins at midnight at her grave

1. *The Willies -Souls of those maidens who die before marriage*
2. *Giselle summoned to do her deed by the Queen of the Willies*
3. *First Hilarian gets it*
4. *Next it's Albrecht's turn*
5. *Giselle saves Albrecht*
6. *Giselle dies again, Albrecht sees the whole thing*
7. *The last gift of flowers*

La Scala notes from Richard Finkelstein, 1996

*

GISELLE f *French, English*
"hostage" or "pledge" from Germanic *gisel.* This is the name of a
well-known ballet by Adolphe Adam

*

It occurred to me you should know me
before you decided to call me or not
It was a lame-brained scheme, though cute,
to have someone give you my phone number
and you not knowing who I am at all,
not even what I look like,
just because I wanted to be cautious
I didn't need to be that cautious
I should've sent you flowers
Or a book . . .

*

LUKE in *English, Biblical* "of Lucania" from Greek *Loukas.*
Lucania was a region in Italy. Saint Luke was the author of the
third Gospel and Acts in the New Testament. Doctor who traveled
in the company of Saint Paul

*

Strange thing

THINKS THE BUDDHA

How we spell Thursday & Thanksgiving
I was born on Thanksgiving
but not on Thursday

*

Being of that generation, I say, "consciousness"

*

I'm writing a novel for Giselle

Giselle Mackenzie

*

By the tennis courts, the neon green balls

THWAP!

Anything but that cold call on the telephone
What a racket!

Serve
Look how hard I can serve

THWAP!

Fig leaves on the coral steps at 6:30 p.m.

This is where I'll hang out
By the pink hibiscus. It's quiet here

I stalk with experience
Those yellow flowers each have a name
I wonder what the flowers call each other

THWAP!

6:45, she's still not down

Someone w/ a headband circles the court
She's not the one

It's the other one, the other Giselle

Blue Jays scream

These trees & asparagus ferns
This congenial botany

I can't wait any longer so I leave

*

I didn't plan to trap Giselle
with the help of the Jockey Club Security Staff

I was downstairs talking to the guard
at the security desk one day

Someone left some fancy brown and gold cigarettes
in my car. It wasn't me

"Really, Joe, I don't think anyone on the staff would
smoke in my car," I say

Maybe it was the guy who parked my car in South Beach
where I went to eat calamari

I complain that someone in security let this woman I met
go up to my apartment without calling me first

She was a nice girl, but married
I sent her home to her husband

"After all, who wants to get gunned down by a
Hare Krishna married to a Latino?"

Joe understood where I was coming from

Hot blooded Buddha

Anyways, Joe promised not to let anyone up to my apartment
without calling me first

He thought I was pretty noble
"Most guys would have taken her for a spin
whether she was married or not." He says, "She looked very nice"

I advanced the discussion

Leaning on the desk, I looked Joe straight in the eye
"Now someone I'd like to meet is Giselle," I say

He thought for a second
"She's very nice. She'd probably be thrilled"

He was ready to call her for me
I had to fill him in on my history with Giselle

"You see, She knows I want to meet her
but doesn't know who I am. She has my phone number . . .
Now promise not to say anything to anyone,
but Ellie called her for me, told her I wanted to meet her
and so on and so forth. And Giselle took my number but hasn't called"

"And you dress good," says Joe. "And she dresses good"
So he proposed another option

"Why don't I call the front gate and tell them to let me know
when she comes through," Joe says. "Then I'll call you in your apartment.
You can come down and meet her"

"Great idea," I say
Petrified at the thought, I began to sweat

"You might have to wait about an hour," Joe says. "She comes in everyday about the same time"

"Oh, God! Okay, I'll do it," I say, "but I'll probably pass out in the elevator"
I run upstairs, change into something clean and decent

Nervous as hell, I pace and pace around the apartment
In ten minutes the phone rings

It's Joe. "She's coming in now"
I run to the elevator. Going down . . .

I stand in front of the security desk waiting to finally meet Giselle
Joe watches the security camera

We wait
And wait

Ellie comes up from the loading dock and sees me
Whispers as she walks by,

>   "Stick around, Giselle will be coming through soon"
>   Ellie's got security cameras too

"What do I do?"
"She's going to go check her mail. Go check your mail
at the same time"

Ellie heads into the mailroom to get out of the way
But Giselle doesn't come
The Condo manager steps out into the lobby, looks around
suspiciously, then disappears back into her office

"Here she comes," says Joe
I don't see her

"She's coming through the front door"
Ellie pops out of the mailroom, heads for the Condo manager's
office and runs into Giselle

Ellie motions with sign language to Giselle that Luke
that's me, Luke, is nearby, to prepare Giselle for the encounter

Giselle walks towards me
I turn and look to Joe and Ellie for moral support and they are gone

Then Giselle beelines to her mail box
I come up behind her leaving lots of space between us

So as not to be threatening
"Hello, Hello," I say. "Giselle, Giselle"

She turns and smiles
"Hi, I'm the guy with the telephone number. I thought
it might be awkward for you to call me. I thought
I should put a face with the number"

"Thank you for introducing yourself," she says
"Can I call you?" I say

"I have your number. Let me call you"
"Will you? Please do"

And Giselle and Giselle and Giselle and
Giselle is off to the elevator, gone upstairs to an unseen
dimension where she blows her nose and snores

Giselle has a very pretty smile
Bright eyes. Pretty lips

The Security Staff returns, congratulate me on my
bravery, action, courage

It was now truly up to Giselle

*

I sense the proximity of a phone call

No phone call

*

You need to powerwalk if you're planning to run late
Giselle was running late

Chameleons courting by the tennis court
Someone shouts, "Vanessa, it's time to go home"

Then what?
Give her 15 minutes more then go to the Luna Star

By the tennis courts
Here's where they walk their under 20lb condominium
regulation size dogs, Lhasas, Chihuahuas
and miniature poodles

White is very popular
Pink hibiscus & those yellow flowers again

No sign of Giselle

*

Luna Star Hangout #2

Brenda "specializes in terrible things"

Two twenty-two year old French students
　　　order a Mochachino Cooler:
　　　　　espresso, chocolate, milk & ice cream

　　　　　　　*

I've done it
No more loitering around the pool
The tennis courts, lobby
Resolve it's truly up to Giselle to decide
if she wants to call me or not
I keep telling myself
Ellie reminds me that this particular story
does not rely upon this *one* Giselle
"There a whole bunch of Giselles out there," she says
"You know what?" I say. "I believe you,
but I don't know how to do it"

　　　　　　　*

Sleep in the afternoon to pass the time
It can't simply be that a lack of companionship is the sole cause for my grief

Mink crow's nest, a marble balcony, the lap of luxury
　　　An anecdote enough for the blues
　　　　　　Giselle can call or not call!

　Toy with medication
Manage vast dimensions of vacant time
Put cactus beside the palm tree
Pink hibiscus over here by the percussionist

The belly dancer's wings woven out of dollar bills

The carpark takes the car for 15 dollars
And returns it with the radio station changed to his kind of music

Janet Reno and Martin Sheen
take pictures on Lincoln Rd. Friday night
She's campaigning for Governor

It's a long way from the White House and "Apocalypse Now"
Or is it?

Some people can talk to anyone anytime
But Luke, the master of shamanic exorcisms, flounders

As the ledge evaporates beneath his feet
his imagination fails to construct stepping stones
through an emotional landscape that could be anyone's condition
Or less

Roaches, raccoons, invasions, fields and basements
    infected with teeming ten-legged horrors

Jealous of what everyone has
Irritated by the good intentioned efforts of dear old friends
Who cheer him on

A bulging bank account assaults his senses
He's moving too slow

His horoscope is not worth writing down
because it tells him what he already knows

Bobbing in the big bucket of sloppy vanity
until old age, blindfolded, carries him away in its perfect teeth

                    *

Luke always worries about something
Therapists don't call back anymore
He considers organizing 70 years of family photos

And Giselle, in the emptiness of ultimate hours, vanishes
on the back roads of insomnia

*

Jacaranda
Dolphins in the Bay

To be Giselle
He's not my type

And so on

*

Gingerly avoiding the subject
Walking around confrontation
The intrusion of resonant presence
Alien face/body in the dust tight laboratory that is home

Giselle's apartment
The introduction of Luke, could possibly be
Giselle's worst fears, the equivalent of introducing
a leaf blower into a Zen monastery

Who desires more, suffers more by absence
Man or Woman come to the cosmic dance equally ill-prepared
It's just a matter of circumstance
That leaves one hungry and the other full

In this case Luke wants more, and Giselle just isn't interested
She thinks Love is silly and Sex embarrassing
We go through it together and apart and learn from our mistakes

"He's not my type"

*

Giselle is 41 years of age
Luke is 50

*

A stoned hippie writing poetry in the Jockey Club
Thinking nobody has faith in anyone but themselves
     unless they're children

*

Dawn returns to the Marble Balcony

Pink Lingerie clings to the dancing nymphets on the pedestal
while bongos, congas, bells, cymbals, fire jugglers wail at Club Touch

There's no place to get a blowjob, no place to work
It's poetry from one end of the cut to the other

I listen to my head, and it's always about Luke, Luke, Luke!
It's not easy being Luke

What are your dreams, Luke?

To finish telling my story

But why can't it end here?

I want to win a Pulitzer prize. For something
Poetry. Fiction. It doesn't matter
I want a reward
Then I can fight to save my fame for history
Otherwise, I will exist only in the pages of some weird anthology
Buried in the archives of a university library

*

Sunday night

June 9, 2002

*

Green parrots on Monday threaten thunderstorms that never come

*

This is the prayer:

Untighten the body to let the Cosmos through

    A cigar boat with a one million mile spew of foaming wake
        It's love

Tides rise, rains fall
Were you expecting company?

*

It's Tuesday
I can't get a job
Mortality's genetic
I keep cheering for Giselle
Toothbrush, hairbrush
Losing hair
It's only 2 o'clock
Moan. Sigh
Spaghetti stain on my sock

*

Giselle passes me in the lobby
I say, Hello

She doesn't acknowledge me
She's busy talking to her daughters walking beside her
"Hello!" Again. She looks up, waves, and keeps walking

Dream Girl, Giselle, shy or deaf, blowing me off
"I don't get that," says Joe. "She never goes out.
I never see her with any men"

*

I had a heavenly time eating pizza
with a shrinking violet from Liverpool
who ratted out her boyfriend
because he leaves hair gel on her pillow
And his dog leaves hair on her bed
and on the floor, which she has to clean
"How tiresome he is!"
But he's well read and fun to go out with
And they laugh together

I'm being followed by a zombie who wants insight,
a key to the mask that makes romance a murder

Where'd those sirens go?

I miss the familiar grumble, rumble, tear, scream of fleshy vehicles
horning, beeping, flashing, singing a sex driven industry
through the tattering throng of storm winds,
rain blown brakes and wheels becoming one engine,
the terminal universe of Giselle, her lips, eyes, determination
to walk in any other direction but mine
Maybe I've got mail

*

Now everyone is angry with Giselle because she ignores me
And she ignores Ellie too

"She used to say hello, now she just runs right into the elevator
You'd think she'd have the courage to say she's not interested"

And Joe was there when I called out a hello to her
He saw her ignore me. He couldn't believe it

"There's a good woman for every good man, I believe that." He says
"Do you?" I say

"Yes, but you have to go out with a lot of them to find the right one"

*

The story goes on to New York

Women friends for dinner
Women friends for museum
Women friends for prayer
Women friends for Luke

*

"Doctor Heal Thyself"

Luke, or is it Philip Whalen, checks into palliative care
unit, where he's lost and afraid,
        approaching the spread of ashes on Mt. Hood

        Nurses expect him to die any day
He can't get out of the corner closing more tightly around him
            It doesn't matter, fortune or fame,

the bladder begins to fail

*

Splashed with a bucket of cold water, he's back on the job
seven stories above Giselle, seven stories below Giselle's father
Endless stories above and below the universal family pantoum

Bride and Groom cut from the top of the sugar white cake frozen for
the glacial age until his father's dead, daughter's pregnant, breasts sag,
and the skin on the heels of her feet begin to crack

Luke's back

from the hospital
putting bandaids on a toothpick, walking
through the enormous puddles engulfing an elegant drive
Healing one moment, ready for the next broken
moment that gets in his way.

THE END: June 13, 2002

4

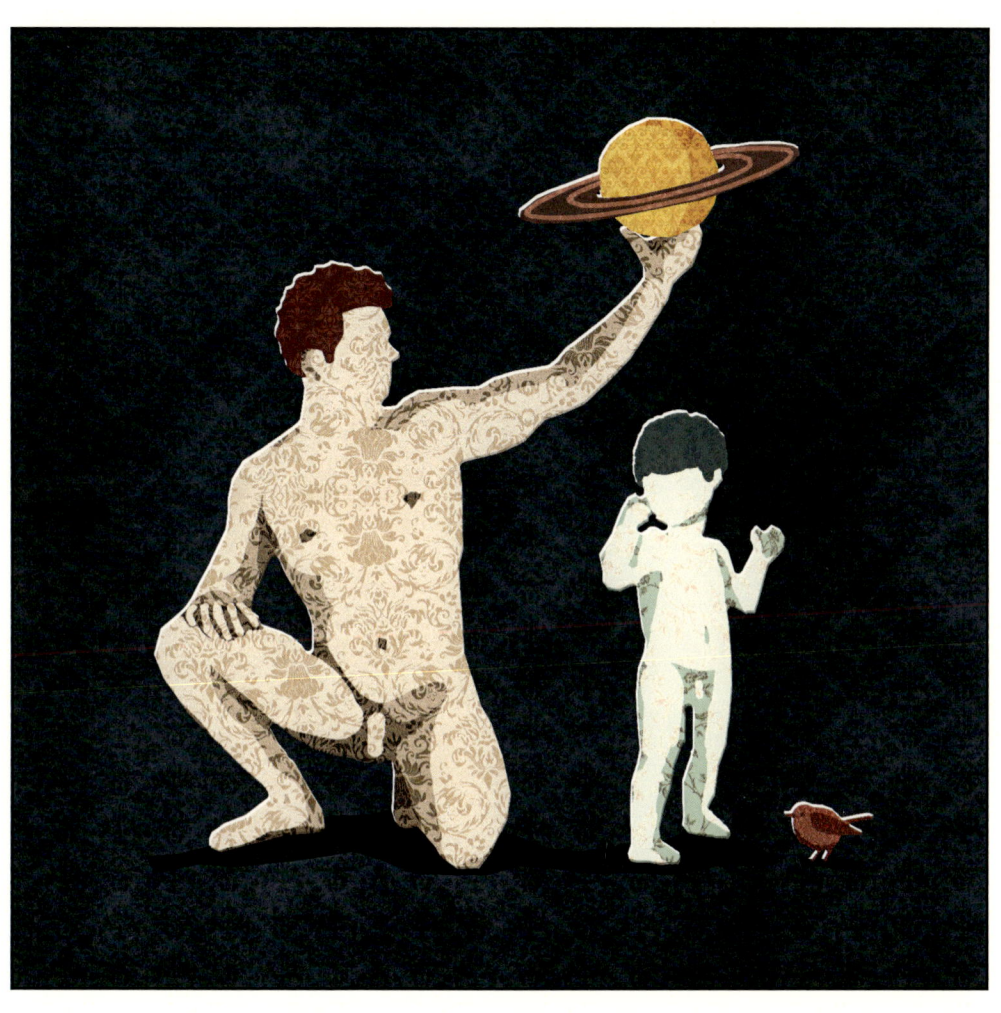

89

HAPPY NEW YEAR FROM THE STARGAZERS

for Terri

1

Looking for Saturn
in the Everglades
Fireflies, clear skies

Red alligator eyes
float in the black canal
by the Miccosukee Reservation

The telescope searches the sky

The moon continues
to be rewarding, but
(sigh) no sign of Saturn

Lost in galaxy chaos
we adjust the lens
Question the technology

Until midnight on the dot
when my son finds a silver ball
Silver rings. Saturn

A million miles away
"I found it, I found it!
Right up there in the sky"

Clear skies, fireflies
Red alligator eyes
We could see Saturn

2

The world can look pretty crappy sometimes

Cars roar down Biscayne Boulevard
Romantic ice cream trucks play the same old music
every century of the world

I want to tell my mother that my best friend has cancer
but my mother is dead

Someone suggests Ionic Footbaths!
Another poet goes to Mexico for his last shot

Zombies and sirens crash through benevolent azure skies
There's no way out but through the front door

From the 9th floor it looks kind of lush
except for a few skyscrapers whoring their way up
through the green canopy

But when you get under the verdure
you see the confusion
Buddhas, flamingos, mezuzahs

and a plaster boy peeing in a koi pond

3

Dear Michael

I have been sitting still for 7 hours.

Love, Louise

4

A pelican flies by my window

I was expecting a buzzard
or a vulture?

What's the difference?
I always forget

My neighbor's lounge chair bangs against the hollow
steel balcony rail above me

I don't want to bury my best friend

A calm in the Mediterranean Sea
We were on a sailboat together unable to get back into port
Then came the mistral

Or when we parked a boat on an Everglades island
Walked around to explore, and returned to find
the boat on dry land. The tide had fallen

It's night, cold
We think we see panthers
"Misty Roses"
Children, yours and mine

5

Dear Michael,

When I don't sit still in a chair, I sit on pillows/etc.

Love, Louise

6

10:31 a.m.
Any minute now, a Renaissance

10:32 a.m., 10:42
I come to the same window confused

A happy helicopter
A quick roaring speedboat with a pinwheel blade
writes on the blue slate of Biscayne Bay

I read the white wake before it settles, fades
Slap, slap, slap against the sea wall

There's meaning in motion, in sound

Woodpeckers say yes, no
Jackhammers say so, so, so

Here comes the dredging barge
So slow
How does it get anywhere?

Another history floats by
Don't let small things get in the way of progress

"Strong chairs make weak asses. Get up!"

Hammer
Hammer
Hammer

7

I write what I see or what passes through my head
These other thoughts rise out of somewhere silent
I'm listening for those

Not Paul Celan

8

If I die now

The death of hands
This white canary

My legacy
My poetry

My land
My car

"This land is my land"

No questions
or prayers without plans

Those lucky stars!

I rattle the pages
I want my muse back

Wind bay history

9

My best friend died today

May 29

10

I can't control my breath by holding it.

5

HURRICANE

The dog is older than me but he has more hair

Strategy   philosophy   aesthetic

Hardwood floors or carpeting?   Kangaroos

Norwegian Rats   Arrive one after another

Holocaust or stubbed toe?   Beyond re-organization

Varieties of Religious Experience

HURRICANE FRANCES
8 AM EDT
MONDAY AUGUST 30, 2004
MAXIMUM WINDS: 120 MPH

At Costco
Bloodshed around the D batteries
Water frenzy (48 bottles)
Garbanzo beans, black beans
Canned apples, peaches, pineapples, peanuts
Oatmeal raisin cookies, muffins
Dublin cheese, cheddar cheese
A crate of tomatoes
Pita (20 count)
Toilet tissue (36 rolls)

Out of retirement into the fire

A frying pan   Existence

Great switcheroo

Just add water   wind   jazz

Chance   reality

Language   perception

Bugaboos

August 31

> On the anniversary of his death
> Alex calls me in my sleep
> Says he's going to temple to pray
> Reprimands me for not calling him more often
> I tell him he's being hard on me

Words from an indelible wave in a Disneyworld vacation video

Alex speaks: *"We're on our way to Typhoon Lagoon.*
We're staying at the Dolphin Hotel!"

With his son Devin and my son Cosmos

Like any other *Wasteland*   *The Bridge*

Crosses *The West*

With a *Howl*   Breath divides

A blood shroud draped over

The face of Mickey Mouse and Daffy Duck

Tiny fractures riddle the feet

Spread to the brain

Immune system   Poetic Life   Flat lines

In Omaha or Miami's summer surf

September 2

**HURRICANE FRANCES
BATTERING TURKS, CAICOS ISLANDS
WINDS: 145 MPH**

*Board up the windows
Move the flowerpots and furniture off the balcony
Evacuate Terri's mom, dog and two blue parakeets*

*Eye-wall close to San Salvador
Big clouds, 20 mph gusts
2.5 million ordered to evacuate*

Word from California, Donald Allen died
Steve's Pizza delivers an eggplant parmigian sandwich

This equals   That plus

Those   Minus the others

At such and such

Pounds per square inch

Suggests

Color can never be

Too bright   Or music

Too loud

Talk to my brother in California about other places to live
Another tropical storm brews off Cape Verde Island

Reports of price gouging: water, plywood, airline tickets

Malls closed: Dadeland, Miami International, Southland,
Westland, Sawgrass, and Aventura

Kennedy Space Center abandoned
Anxiety (not barometric pressure) may induce labor

Chocolate cake & diet cola

Alex speaks: "*This is the view from our bedroom window.*

Over there is The Disney Boardwalk.
Which is kind of neat."

Alex doesn't care Disney World has become The Culture

Code   narrative   lyric moving

Likewise dissimilar   It can be   That palm

Swale   arch   Father   claw   wire

That's what I'm in it for

September 3

> **Hurricane Frances, eye slightly weakened,**
> **edges tattered, expected to regain focus**
> **as it crosses over The Bahamas**

Feeder bands blow leaves 9 stories up onto balcony

> **Frances comes on the heels of Hurricane Charley,**
> **which hit on Aug. 13 with 145 mph winds,**
> **knocking out power to hundreds of thousands**
> **and causing 27 deaths as it crossed**
> **from the Gulf of Mexico into the Atlantic.**

Red   veal   Red apple   tart   Red   Red . . .

Alex instructs illegal immigrants on how
To circumvent immigration laws
Become US citizens for a few hundred dollars
Grandfathered in under amnesty clause
"There's no way to close the border," he says.
"And Someone's going to get paid to help these huddled masses."
It's a larcenous world but he believes in what he's doing

Red high heels   Red lipstick   short Red skirts

Polka dot panties   Red   Red . . .

The Red-cheeked baby girl

He named after himself   Dark-haired boy

He named after a Red cliff above a Red sea

Frizzy Red dog monogrammed A.G.

Red   pizza from P3's Madrid

Red rocks   scotch on the rocks

Picasso rendering   Of Red dreams

Red canvas   Magritte   Big Red sunset

On Mediterranean beach

Scandalous   Red   amorous   Red

Money   status   beautimous   Red

Red sails in a mid-day lull

Red winds blow from the Red

Continent of Africa

Storm shutters rattle and flex
Terri makes spaghetti
Maybe it's time to leave Florida before Florida leaves itself.

Alex speaks: *"Good Morning, Michael.*
                 Cosmos, say hello!
                 Devin!
                 The four banditos!"

Blue Fiat Spider masquerades as Lamborghini

Blue lungs   Waves   Blue cells swell

Flood white sheets in steel Blue rooms

Blue disinfectant fumes   Blue infection

Blue peel and eat shrimp

Masquerade as mashed potatoes   Meatloaf

Blue straw drains juice of Blue universe

Blue fire burns through Blue steel   Mirrors

That's who we're becoming   Blue

Blue mornings on the Interstate

In those Blue Carolinas   Where we wrestled

In drifts of Blue snow

Blue elementals   Chinese Blue

A best friends' Blue adventure   Blue

Years that never came and stayed

In a Blue forever

September 4

Wake up and check the news
Wind & rain in The Bahamas
Marsh Harbor
Power out
Sky full gray
Alex is dead

If I name them they're unknown

Every cell and screw   Together webbed

Did I hear you say rain?

Any minute now   Questions

Did I hear you say blue?

It should be   white   Stars and Stripes

Public Trust   Anarchy   White washed

White woolen wishes whirling woe

Whatever punches a hole in The Ideal

I can live without this   Ideal

System   branch   rat   root   hand

What it offers   Tongue twitch

White   Wings   Worlds   Whispers

White   Improvisations

Take over the page

The dog has no where to pee except on the white carpet
The storm moves painfully slow
Outer bands of wind and rain whip Florida near Jupiter
2 men arrested for trying to break into a church

Power out
No TV
Shirtless barefoot man in shorts 9 stories below
walks in the wind blowing around his house

Palm fronds twist
Ficus leaves flap

There's life after T.V.
"I knew that," Terri says.

There's wind, clouds, glyphs on Biscayne Bay
"Glyphs? What are glyphs?"

Hieroglyphics
"Oh."

Power returns
The Spanish newscaster describes the hurricane as,
"Zig-zag-iando."

Post-modern psychosis

Collage

Nose evolves into feet

Fingers become ears   A-Bombs

Engraved invitations   A second wedding

Bride in white   Groom in torn blue jeans

Slice of banana   Custom built house

The marriage is a blast   Help!

U.S.A. eavesdrops through pristine stage walls

Projects Yesterday   Today   and   Tomorrow

Land   A Political Theme Park Nation

We have a good time   wherever we go

Rain ghosts whoosh by

Let's do an exquisite corpse
"I'm not in the mood," Terri says.

Tree with a tree house blows down
Predictions of 6 to 20 inches of rain

FRANCES ARRIVES

I refuse to gender a hurricane
Bitch!
Welcome to America
Bigger than Immigration and Naturalization Service
Track it!

Alex speaks: *"Michael and I are achy from floating*
                    around the Typhoon Lagoon."

Rats scratch at gardenias

Whatever does it mean?

The dog sleeps with his nose at the door

I believe in Alex

Conditions favorable for tornadoes
Frances comes ashore at Sewall Point
It's me against God & Nature

"It's the end of the world," Terri says.

September 5

Morning
Windy & messy
Blows from S. S. E.

In Orlando
Mickey Mouse & Goofy batten down the hatches

The following people will not be accepted into my club:

Dead poets   living poets   dead or living artists

Politicians   auto mechanics   insurance salesman   soldiers

True-believers   critics   television and movie actors

Kenny   Kyle   Butters   criminals

Card carrying members of international health organizations

Factory workers   music movie industry personnel

Executives   anyone for hire

Electronic equipment manufacturers

Tech support   slave owners   Santa Claus

Little Orphan Annie   pharmacists   alchemists

Philologists   psychologists   psychiatrists   matchmakers

Interior decorators   activists

Pacifists   mathematicians   biologists   other physicists

Donald Duck   farmers   shepherds   groomers

Cosmeticians   Butchers   bakers   Bart Simpson

Fakirs Home care providers   casketeers   novelists

Editors   auditors   court reporters   judges   clowns

Seal   whale   poodle   dolphin   parrot trainers

Saints   gymnasts   co-dependents

Co-defendants   co-conspirators

"Co-co-ri-co"

And foreigners   unless they pay me a dollar

Frances, a thousand miles across
moves over the center of the state
headed for the Gulf of Mexico

Some shredded roofs, uprooted trees
Mandatory evacuation lifted
50 mph gusts

3 million people still in the dark

I'm sorry everyone isn't having fun because

There are all kinds of fun things to do

Bake walnut   banana muffins

Have a beer   play with the dog

Smile   Damn you   Smile!

You get what you ask for whether you ask for it or not

"It's just a matter of patience," said Bishop G. A. White,
Pastor of the Ft. Pierce Church of the Living God.
"Wait on the Lord and wait on the weather."

    HURRICANE IVAN
    1,210 MILES EAST-SOUTHEAST OF LESSER ANTILLES

Hurricane Gods bowl for Miami
"This time we'll do it right."
Weather forecasters track possibilities of

IVAN

Something to upset our lives
so we don't have to think about
what really upsets us

Salty oranges

A Survivalist's Guide to Mushrooms

It's winter and according to zoologists

I'm human

In bed   feet propped on the pillows

Left arm rests on the windowsill

Right arm rests on the rock

Fingers dangle in the creek

Head turned inside out

I don't need the moon   In the dark

I stand over the toilet   Pray

The plumbing works

Squalls . . .

Urban Flood Advisory

Squalls . . .

Someone tries to return used plywood to lumber store

> . . .wind and water whacked swaths of southern Florida
> with fire-hose force Sunday, submerging entire roadways
> and tearing off rooftops even as the storm weakened
> and crawled inland with heavy rains in its wake.

Blue sky.   Gray sky

Field Guide to Embolisms

President's Domestic Spy Program

"Live by the gun   die by the gun"

And other quaint sayings

Live oak   Madrone

Mushrooms for making cookies

Or dying your dog yellow

Inducing hallucinations

These are facts

Steak sandwich at Woody's

Across from Publix on Biscayne Blvd.

What did Alex and I talk about?

Blue sky   Gray sky

Isn't it incredible?

Squalls . . .

This is an opportunity for George Bush
to reach out as father-provider to destitute survivors
of Hurricane whichever-it-was
Frances? Ivan? Alpha? Beta? Dogma?

Power Out: 6:25 p.m.
Power On: 6:25 p.m.

Alex speaks: "Here we are eating at the Disney Boardwalk."

Infra-verbal   hyper-graphic   Zen

Marxist Capitalism

Fundamentalist   Pornography

Rain gathers in sags

Garbage pick-up today   Tuesday

Jean Cocteau's *Orpheus Trilogy*

Alex liked John Grisham novels

117

And surfing at dawn

September 6

Frances in Gulf of Mexico threatens Florida panhandle

huge spiraling counter-clockwise countenance

WINDS 65 MPH
5-10 INCH RAINS
DRIFITING NORTHWESTERLY

Alex speaks: *"We can see the fireworks at Epcot from here."*

I've lost my sandalwood prayer beads

Behind the washing machine

Alex's dream:

Watch television from bunk bed

In a yacht anchored in Gulf Stream

My dream:

Give up angst

Live in a cabin in the redwoods

But first   The Passage   Rings of Hell

118

Ten thousand reincarnations

Worlds   worlds   worm-world

Wolf-world   Queen-world   mastodon-world

Chihuahua-world

Fire   flood   hurricane-world

Disney World

And if that isn't BAD enough

There's Universal Studios

Enough beans, batteries and water
to get through another storm
that almost arrives

IVAN

485 MILES EAST-SOUTHEAST OF BARBADOS

Lovers don't need to have a President in common

Or share a bathroom

I sat in bed with a bass guitar

At Virginia St. Apartments in Coconut Grove

Played the same three notes

119

Over and over until Alex came

Bursting through the door, "I'm trying to study!"

Truth is he had a girl in his bedroom

And I was throwing off his rhythm

Praise be to Ahmad Jamal for that three-note memory

That's all you need   three notes

And love goes on

Alex, in yellow flowered shirt,
poses on Disney Boardwalk eating a burger
Sipping a Margarita

Alex speaks: "*. . .and taking Vicodin.*"

Miami Beach *stetl*

Alex and me, 1960

show off our waist length hair

at Hal's Delicatessen

Alex floats on his back in the waterpark all day
He feels a hundred years old

Alex speaks: "*I feel 105 years old.*"

Chewing gum, twinkle in his eye
He stares into the camera

Alex and I cross the Atlantic Ocean

From New York to Cannes

With an unscheduled stop in Naples

The ship   The Michelangelo

Diverted because of cholera

September 9

IVAN
CATEGORY 5
WEST-NORTHWEST OR 295 DEGREES AT 13 KT
HEADED FOR JAMAICA

Alex speaks: *"We're on the tram to Disney World."*

Purple-Staining Bearded Milk Cap

Poison Pie mushroom

California Sister

Hereditaments and appurtenances

TO HAVE AND TO HOLD

Document and notarize quotidian

Eat unsalted roasted peanuts

One for me   one for the dog   two for me

One for the dog   etc.

September 10

Alex speaks: "We're at the Disney entrance!"

Scarlet Waxy Cap

Redwood Rooter

Fetid Adder's Tongue

Deer mushroom

"Pittsburgh Penguins May Be for Sale"

March of the Penguins

Penguins Anonymous

I acknowledge what I deny

Steady breathing helps   SPACE

Popcorn for dinner   IDEA

I don't like to be pigeonholed   YAWN

Hieronymus Bosch Does Guerneville

Other people believe in Andy Kaufman

HURRICANE IVAN ADVISORY NUMBER 33
GRADUALLY APPROACHING JAMAICA . . .
AT 11 AM EDT . . . GOVERNMENT OF CUBA
ISSUES HURRICANE WATCH . . .
DANGEROUS BATTERING WAVES . . .
POSSIBLY CAUSING LIFE- THREATENING
FLASH FLOODS AND MUD SLIDES . . .

Alex speaks: *"Now we're going into Tomorrow Land."*

Uncle Paul evacuates Naples, FL

September 11

. . .DRIFTING WESTWARD

The Wonders of India

The Art of Ancient China

The Autobiography of Katherine Hepburn

I choose a season

Winter 2006

I see this   I'm here   and then   I'm here

"Probability of Ivan hitting Miami less than 1 percent"

September 12

BULL BAY, Jamaica - Hurricane Ivan strengthened
to a rare Category 5 storm capable of catastrophic damage,
leaving Jamaica and aiming for the Cayman Islands
with winds reaching 165 mph, the U.S. National Hurricane
Center said Saturday. Ivan has killed 56 people across
the Caribbean so far this week, including 34 in Grenada
and 11 in Jamaica. Millions more people are in its path,
with Ivan projected to go between the Cayman Islands,
make a direct hit on Cuba and then either move into
the Gulf of Mexico or hit South Florida.

If God doesn't help us, I think this is going to be extremely
tragic," said Maria del Carmen Boza, a 65-year-old resident
of Cojimar, a seaside community in Cuba once frequented
by Ernest Hemingway. "All of Cuba is worried. This
looks like it's going to be really dangerous.

President Fidel Castro sought to assuage such concerns.
Saturday night on state television, Castro said, his
government had mobilized to save lives and property.
"This country is prepared to face this hurricane."

Yellow   Yellow   Yellow   wall

Unidentified mushroom on dining table

(might be the head of a porn star)

Yellow pages

Ft. Lauderdale   Boca Raton   Delray Beach

White ceramic cow   Digital camera

Anime and cola   There's always a better world

If you are compelled to wish

Alex, wherever you are, *if* you are, *don't* wish

Stand on the sun   Let the coffin steam!

And so the peacock lives

At the local dump   Butterflies in the zoo

Gnomes   Undines   Sylphs and Salamanders

In the sketch you made

Magma   manna   mud

Ice storm   earthquake   spontaneous

Combustion   Theophrastus Philippus Aureolus

Bombastus von Hohenheim . . .   "The dose makes the poison"

I paint the very yellow wall with *another* coat of yellow

September 13

Alex speaks: *"In line to The Haunted House.*
We're getting a Fast Pass to Splash Mountain.
Ho, ho, ho, it's a pirate's life for me!"

Ride the wind, shoot from the hip
Kids in the gift shop play swashbuckler

"Careful of the eyes."

"They're buyin', they're shoppin',
They're movin', they're groovin'."

Devin points the camera at Alex

"Dad, Say Hello!"

"Hello."

"Say something else."

"I love you Devin."

Not even places of worship were spared the wrath of Ivan

When I was young

Death was something

126

I could do to myself

Now it's something

that can happen to me

Alex speaks: *"It's a Small World after all . . . "*

We're also concerned about flooding in Fulton County

Alex speaks: *"There goes Michael to the bathroom again, fourth time today.*
            He knows every restroom in Disney World."

The tally of tornadoes growing

Alex speaks: *"The things we do for our kids*
            How many boats do they have in this ride?"

            "Though the mountains divide
            And the oceans are wide
            It's a small, small world."

Rollercoaster boatloads of kids
shoot over mountainside & scream
We wait to take pictures of our children

I slap Alex on the arm,

            "Did you see that girl, Alex?"

"Stop looking at the girls, Michael."

. . .cloud, lightning, leaf, gum wrapper, carport canopy
shred, limbs, fence, hair
. . .pin curtain shut so morning won't come in
. . .shorten length of waiting awake, lengthen
time I can dream of times to come

Death Hurricane
The fan above my bed reminds me
I'm not where I think I am

"What's for dinner, Terri?"
"Blah!"

"How about we share an apple?"
"Blah!"

Ivan lands in Mobile

It's a scary-looking hammer knocker," said 57-year-old Billy Porter, a building contractor who was gearing up for a day of fishing. Porter said he's prepared to ride out the storm at his log house about 4 miles from the water. "I've got a generator for my TV - as long I've got my TV, I'm all right," he said.

September 15, 2004

Alex speaks: *"Now we're at Universal Studios!"*

We're in a movie. Dr. Seuss Land, Spiderman . . .

TROPICAL STORM JEANNE
WINDS 55 KT, GUSTS TO 65 KT

HURRICANE WARNING IN EFFECT
FOR PUERTO RICO AND U.S. VIRGIN ISLANDS
TROPICAL STORM WARNING
REMAINS IN EFFECT
FOR BRITISH VIRGIN ISLANDS . . .
ST. KITTS . . .

Alex points at Big Twister Roller Coaster at Universal

Alex speaks: "This is what they're going on, these crazy kids."

September 16, 2004

Buildings gone in a rain shroud

Turn on Weather Channel

JEANNE BECOMES A HURRICANE . . .

Alex turns the camera off.

August 30, 2004, revised in Hollywood, FL
on the eve of Katrina, 2005

129

About the Author

Michael Rothenberg is a poet, editor and publisher of the online literary magazine BigBridge.org, co-founder of 100 Thousand Poets for Change (www.100tpc.org) and co-founder of Poets In Need.

Born in Miami Beach, Florida in 1951, Rothenberg moved to the San Francisco Bay Area in 1975 and co-founded Shelldance Orchid Gardens in Pacifica, which is dedicated to the cultivation of orchids and bromeliads. While in Pacifica, he helped lead local environmental actions that stopped major coastal developments that would destroy wildlife habitat.

He has published 19 books of poetry including *Nightmare of The Violins, Favorite Songs, Man/Woman* (a collaboration with Joanne Kyger), *Unhurried Vision, Monk Daddy, The Paris Journals, Choose, My Youth As A Train, Murder,* and *Sapodilla* (Editions du Cygne-Swan World, Paris, France, 2016). *Indefinite Detention: A Dog Story*, was published in 2013 by Ekstasis Editions (Victoria, B.C., Canada), and in 2014 by Shabda Press (USA). A Spanish/English edition of *Indefinite Detention: A Dog Story*, and the poetic journal collection, *Tally Ho and the Cowboy Dream/The Real and False Journals: Book 5* are scheduled for publication in 2017 by Varasek Ediciones (Madrid, Spain).

His work has been published widely in literary reviews and

included in anthologies such as *Ecopoetry: A Contemporary American Anthology,* edited by Ann Fisher-Wirth and Laura-Gray Street (Trinity University Press), *43 Poetas por Ayotzinapa,* edited by Jesús González Alcántara and Moisés H. Cortés Cruz (Mexico), *Saints of Hysteria, A Half-Century of Collaborative American Poetry,* edited by David Trinidad and Denise Duhamel (Soft Skull Press), *Hidden Agendas/Unreported Poetics,* edited by Louis Armand (Litteraria Pragensia), and *For the Time-Being: The Bootstrap Book of Poetic Journals,* edited by Tyler Doherty and Tom Morgan (Bootstrap Productions).

His editorial work includes several volumes in the Penguin Poets series: *Overtime* by Philip Whalen, *As Ever* by Joanne Kyger, *David's Copy* by David Meltzer, and *Way More West* by Ed Dorn. He is also editor of *The Collected Poems of Philip Whalen* published by Wesleyan University Press.

Rothenberg currently lives on Lake Jackson in Tallahassee, Florida.

About the Artist

Donatella D'Angelo is a photographer and graphic design-er from Milan, Italy who has been working in the visual arts since the 1980's. In recent years, she turned her focus to the photographic investigation of "body and identity." Her photos and collages have been exhibited in several European galleries, including Galleria Scoglia di Quarto (Milan-Italy) and Trien-nal Eupropeene de L'Estampe Contemporaaine, Castelsarrasin (Toulouse-France), as well as in the USA at The Empty Spaces Gallery (Putnam, CT). He work has also appeared in various online and print publications such as *Style:* "Corriere della Sera", *Night Italia:* "AnarChic", *Il Foglio Clandestino, The Woven Tale Press* Vol. III #8, *Il Verri:* "Gli eccessi dell'io", and others. She received the first place prize at the national contest LABirinti-FOTOgrafia 2015.

www.donatelladangelo7.tumblr.com/
www.donatelladangelo.wix.com/photography
http://donatelladangelo.wix.com/illustrations

BOOKS BY DOS MADRES PRESS

◗ 2004

Annie Finch - *Home Birth*

Norman Finkelstein - *An Assembly*

Richard Hague - *Burst, Poems Quickly*

Robert Murphy - *Not For You Alone*

Tyrone Williams - *Futures, Elections*

◗ 2005

Gerry Grubbs - *Still Life*

James Hogan - *Rue St. Jacques*

Peter O'Leary - *A Mystical Theology of the Limbic Fissure*

David Schloss - *Behind the Eyes*

Henry Weinfield - *The Tears of the Muses*

◗ 2006

Paul Bray - *Things Past and Things to Come*

Michael Heller - *A Look at the Door with the Hinges Off*

Michael Heller - *Earth and Cave*

Richard Luftig - *Off The Map*

J. Morris - *The Musician, Approaching Sleep*

◗ 2007

Joseph Donahue - *The Copper Scroll*

Pauletta Hansel - *First Person*

Burt Kimmelman - *There Are Words*

Robert Murphy - *Life in the Ordovician*

William Schickel - *What A Woman*

◗ 2008

Michael Autrey - *From The Genre Of Silence*

Paul Bray - *Terrible Woods*

Eric Hoffman - *Life At Braintree*

Henry Weinfield - *Without Mythologies*

❯2009

Jon Curley - *New Shadows*

Deborah Diemont - *Wanderer*

Norman Finkelstein - *Scribe*

Nathan Swartzendruber - *Opaque Projectionist*

❯2010

Gerry Grubbs - *Girls in Bright Dresses Dancing*

Michael Henson - *The Tao of Longing & The Body Geographic*

Keith Holyoak - *My Minotaur*

Madeline Tiger - *The Atheist's Prayer*

Donald Wellman - *A North Atlantic Wall*

❯2011

Pauletta Hansel - *What I Did There*

Eric Hoffman - *The American Eye*

David M. Katz - *Claims of Home*

Burt Kimmelman - *The Way We Live*

Bea Opengart - *In The Land*

David A. Petreman - *Candlelight in Quintero-bilingual ed.*

Paul Pines - *Reflections in a Smoking Mirror*

Murray Shugars - *Songs My Mother Never Taught Me*

Madeline Tiger - *From the Viewing Stand*

James Tolan - *Red Walls*

Martin Willetts Jr. - *Secrets No One Must Talk About*

Tyrone Williams - *Adventures of Pi*

❯2012

Jennifer Arin - *Ways We Hold*

Jon Curley - *Angles of Incidents*

Sara Dailey - *Earlier Lives*

Richard Darabaner - *Plaint*

Deborah Diemont - *Diverting Angels*

Richard Hague - *During The Recent Extinctions*
R. Nemo Hill - *When Men Bow Down*
W. Nick Hill - *And We'd Understand Crows Laughing*
Keith Holyoak - *Foreigner*
Pamela L. Laskin - *Plagiarist*
Austin MacRae - *The Organ Builder*
Rick Mullin - *Soutine*
Pam O'Brien - *The Answer To Each Is The Same*
Lianne Spidel & Anne Loveland - *Pairings*
Henry Weinfield - *A Wandering Aramaean*
Donald Wellman - T*he Cranberry Island Series*
Anne Whitehouse - *The Refrain*

❧2013

Mary Margaret Alvarado - *Hey Folly*
John Anson - *Jose-Maria de Heredia's Les Trophées*
Gerry Grubbs - *The Hive-a book we read for its honey*
Ruth D. Handel - *Tugboat Warrior*
Eric Hoffman - *By the Hours*
Nancy Kassell - *Text(isles)*
Sherry Kearns - *Deep Kiss*
Owen Lewis - *Sometimes Full of Daylight*
Mario Markus - *Chemical Poems-One For Each Element*
Rick Mullin - *Coelacanth*
Robert Murphy - *From Behind The Blind*
Paul Pines - *New Orleans Variations & Paris Ouroboros*
Murray Shugars - *Snakebit Kudzu*
Jason Shulman - *What does reward bring you but to bind you
    to Heaven like a slave?*
Olivia Stiffler - *Otherwise, we are safe*
Carole Stone - *Hurt, the Shadow-the Josephine Hopper poems*
Brian Volck - *Flesh Becomes Word*
Kip Zegers - *The Poet of Schools*

❭ 2014

John Anson - *Time Pieces - poems & translations*
Ann Cefola - *Face Painting in the Dark*
Grace Curtis - *The Shape of a Box*
Dennis Daly - *Nightwalking with Nathaniel-poems of Salem*
Karen George - *Swim Your Way Back*
Ralph La Charity - *Farewellia a la Aralee*
Patricia Monaghan - *Mary-A Life in Verse*
Rick Mullin - *Sonnets on the Voyage of the Beagle*
Fred Muratori - *A Civilization*
Paul Pines - *Fishing on the Pole Star*
Don Schofield - *In Lands Imagination Favors*
Daniel Shapiro - *The Red Handkerchief and other poems*
Maxine Silverman - *Palimpsest*
Lianne Spidel & Anne Loveland - *A Bird in the Hand*
Sarah White - *The Unknowing Muse*

❭ 2015

Stuart Bartow - *Einstein's Lawn*
Kevin Cutrer - *Lord's Own Anointed*
Richard Hague - *Where Drunk Men Go*
Ruth D. Handel - *No Border is Perennial*
Pauletta Hansel - *Tangle*
Eric Hoffman - *Forms of Life*
Roald Hoffmann - *Something That Belongs To You*
Keith Holyoak - *The Gospel According to Judas*
David M. Katz - *Stanzas on Oz*
Sherry Kearns - *The Magnificence of Ruin*
Marjorie Deiter Keyishian - *Ashes and All*
Jill Kelly Koren - *The Work of the Body*
Owen Lewis - *Best Man*
Rick Mullin - *Stignatz & the User of Vicenza*
Paul Pines - *Message from the Memoirist*

Quanita Roberson - *Soul Growing-Wisdom for thirteen year old boys from men around the world*

David Schloss - *Reports from Babylon and Beyond*

Eileen R. Tabios - *INVENT[ST]ORY Selected Catalog Poems & New 1996-2015*

Kip Zegers - *The Pond in Room 318*

❯2016

Eduardo Chirinos - *Still Life with Flies [naturaleza muerta con moscas]*, Bilingual, English translation by G. J. Racz

Norman Finkelstein - *The Ratio of Reason to Magic: New & Selected Poems*

Gerry Grubbs - *The Palace of Flowers*

R. Nemo Hill - *In No Man's Ear*

W. Nick Hill - *Blue Nocturne*

Sharon Olinka - *Old Ballerina Club*

Natalie Safir - *Eyewitness*

Geoffrey Woolf - *Learn to Love Explosives*

David Almaleck Wolinsky - *The Crane is Flying - Early Poems*

www.dosmadres.com